SO-AJZ-320

CORVINA PRESS

Hungary

1 Budapest. Hotel Budapest
2 Transdanubian peasant house
3 The southern gate tower of Buda Castle
   with the Inner City in the background
4 Budapest. Sign of the one-time Red Hedgehog
   Inn in the Castle District
5 Budapest. Fortuna Street in the Castle District
6 Budapest. Matthias Church at night
7–8 Budapest. The Elizabeth Bridge
9 Budapest. View of the Chain Bridge with
   the Parliament building in the background
10 Szentendre. Houses
11 Szentendre. Marx Square
12 Szentendre. Roofs
13 The Danube at Visegrád
14 Landscape near Visegrád
15 Visegrád. King Matthias's coat of arms on the red
   marble well in his former palace (15th century)
16 Visegrád. Solomon's Tower (13th century)
17 Esztergom. The Baroque Church of the Watertown
   with the Cathedral (19th century) on Castle
   Hill and the ruins of the Royal Palace of the Árpád
   dynasty (11–13th century) in the background
18 Esztergom. A medieval wooden statue
   in the Cathedral
19–20 Fertőd. The former Esterházy Palace
   (18th century)
21 Győr. Modern house in the city centre
22 Bank of the Danube, still life
23 Preparing dinner
24 Trade sign in Kőszeg
25 Kőszeg. Jurisich Castle (15–16th century)
26 Kőszeg. Courtyard of the Town Hall
   (15–17th century)
27 Sopron. Knocker on the entrance
   of the Storno House (17th century)

28 Sopron. Statue of the Holy Trinity on
   Beloiannisz Square (17th century)
29 View of Sopron with the former
   Benedictine Church in the centre (13th century)
30 Sopron. The courtyard of the Fabricius House
   (17th century)
31 Sopron. Gothic house in Új Street
32–35 The Church of Ják (13th century)
36 Veszprém. The Bishop's Palace (18th century)
37 The Castle of Veszprém (14–16th century)
38 Százhalombatta. The Danube Oil Refinery
39 Székesfehérvár. Hotel Alba Regia
40 Székesfehérvár. I. István Square
41 Martonvásár. The former Brunszvik mansion
42 Bust of Beethoven in the mansion's garden
43 Stork's nest
44 Tác. Roman tomb
45 The Castle of Sümeg (13–16th century)
46 The Castle of Nagyvázsony (15–16th century)
47 Turkish warrior in the tournament at Nagyvázsony
48–50 Lake Balaton
51 After the regatta
52 Sunset
53 The towers of Tihany Abbey
54 St. Jerome on the pulpit of the Abbey Church
   (18th century)
55 The organ of the Abbey Church (18th century)
56 The crypt (11th century) with the tomb
   of the Hungarian king Andrew I
57 Badacsony
58 Badacsony. Róza Szegedy's house
59 Badacsony vineyard
60 Autumn at Lake Balaton
61 Pécs. Cathedral
62 Pécs. Twelfth century statue from the Cathedral
63 Scene from the "Busó" Carnival in Mohács

Hungary

Confession of a Lyricist

Hungary is a small country, but as her friends abroad often say, she is a great power in three fields: music, mathematics and lyric poetry. Looking at the delightful colours in Károly Gink's photographs of Hungary's regions and towns, I think that perhaps it is not too pretentious for a native of the country to add a fourth one: photographic art. Photography has the advantage of music and mathematics, it can be understood without recourse to language, while we can still only give our word of honour as to the greatness and universal appeal of Hungarian lyric poetry, our greatest pride; although in the last ten years it has found such translators as Guillevic, Martinov, Hermlin, Fühmann, Ted Hughes and Edwin Morgan.

A Hungarian man of letters cannot speak of photographs without mentioning his prides and sorrows in the same breath. I do so at this time because of the inspiration of Károly Gink's photographs. They evoke in one's mind the beauty of the Hungarian towns and countryside. At the same time they affect one as deeply as only poetry can. Gink has joined the line of our fourth "great power" in which stand the artists Brassai, Capa, Aladár Székely, Márton Munkácsi, Károly Escher and Kata Kálmán. Among them there are dramatists of the camera like Capa, epic poets like Székely, satirists, of course, like Brassai, and lyricists—which in some sense they all are, because they are Hungarian. Photographic lyricism is the specific artistic idiom of Károly Gink, and in this volume his characteristic style comes forth in his use of soft, rich colours.

If art can be defined as reality seen by and filtered through a given temperament, the definition nowhere becomes so valid as in photographic art. A photographer's reality is the most natural, full-blooded, palpable, the least transposed, the most direct reality. This becomes evident in this volume. However, just because the presence of reality is so palpable, a lyric temperament is necessary for the alchemy of art to take place. I do not have to prove that this has taken place in Károly Gink's pictures; his eighty photographs speak for themselves. This volume is the confession of a lyricist of how and what he sees in Hungary and what he brings to it from his own self. He brings his sensitivity, which is much more delicate than that of the emulsion on his film.

I believe Gink has taken stock of what he liked best in his country, what he has liked for a long time, perhaps since his childhood. He takes a good look at it from every direction. Then he sets the aperture of his eyes, consults his memories for timing, measures distance against his emotions, and only then does he pick up his camera. In this way, filtered, as it were, through his temperament, he notices the two gentle beasts in a side-wall of the Romanesque church of Ják. In this way he goes back to the one-time Roman province, Pannonia, to the village of Tác, once called Gorsium, and gives homage to the memory of the ancestors in his photograph of a stele depicting father and son.

Just as Gink's camera rediscovers his native land, so we discover, looking at his pictures, the structure of his book. Here too he remains faithful to poetry, for poetry is the strictest genre. Gink's volume has both an inner and an outer structure. The latter can more easily be discovered. He starts out from Budapest (where else could he have started from?), turns towards the north, along the Danube, to Szentendre, Visegrád, Esztergom, and from there to the western gate of the country, Fertőd, the one-time Eszterháza, and the Castle of Kőszeg. On the road of centuries and the route of today's tourists, he then arrives in Sopron, and makes a detour to Ják.

Then he heads south, to Veszprém, *urbs reginae*: once the town of the queens of the Árpád dynasty. After Székesfehérvár he makes a trip to the bust of Beethoven on the island of music in Martonvásár. The castles of Sümeg and Nagyvázsony remind one of Hungary's stormy past. At Lake Balaton he is fascinated by the beauty of Tihany and the majesty of the Badacsony. Crossing the Transdanubian hills he reaches the town of Pécs with its flowers and cathedral. At Mohács, finally, he crosses the Danube and with a giant step he arrives in Debrecen. He loves the Hortobágy so much that he can say something new even about this over-photographed region. However, he is unkind to the eastern part of the country; he only glances at the towns of Eger, Miskolc and Salgótarján. I could show him beautiful colours, regions and towns in the County of Zemplén as well, but this volume is his lyrical confession, not mine.

His tour of Hungary through photography forms the outer structure of the book. The inner becomes evident in the fact that his photographs present Hungarian architecture. Romanesque architecture is represented, apart from Ják, by both Pécs and the towers of Buda Castle, as well as by the thick columns and the royal tomb in the crypt of Tihany Abbey. Gothic architecture is portrayed in pictures from Esztergom and Sopron. Gink also captures the Hungarian Renaissance, which is synonymous with the name of King Matthias. According to a papal legate, on feast days red wine used to flow from his red marble fountain in Visegrád. Gink, unlike others endowed with a snobbish fastidiousness, loves the rich Hungarian Baroque period, a fact which makes his books especially dear to me. His angle of the Esterházy Palace at Fertőd may not be very original, nevertheless he makes us see all that is essential to it. His portrayal of the "peasant" Baroque style in Tihany and Badacsony, however, is both original and intimate. After Classicist Székesfehérvár the Rococo of Szentendre enchants us. Finally, keeping the proportions of history and art history in view, we are shown the steel, iron and glass architecture of our age: the gracile Elizabeth Bridge in Budapest, Hotel Alba Regia in Székesfehérvár, which harmonizes well with its older surroundings, and the chimneys of Salgótarján. In a second edition, however, I would also welcome photographs of this town's new, organically designed, elegant and modern centre. This small criticism is my only critical confession about Gink's rich lyrical confession—a lyricist's confession of his love for his country.

Iván Boldizsár

© Károly Gink 1976 · Design by István Murányi
The photographs were taken with a Hasselblad camera and a Zeiss lens.
ISBN 963 13 4641 2
Printed in Hungary, 1976 · Kossuth Printing House, Budapest · CO1232–h–7680

Károly Gink

Hungary

**Towns and
the Countryside
Preface by
Iván Boldizsár**

Corvina Press

57, 58, 59